INSPIRATION

from Above

A Collection of Poems, Prayers, & Thoughts

Lana Keller

ISBN 979-8-89309-660-6 (Paperback)
ISBN 979-8-89309-661-3 (Digital)

Covenant Books
11661 Hwy 707
Murrells Inlet, SC 29576
www.covenantbooks.com

Dedication

Dad's Poetic Legacy

First, I would like to thank Jesus Christ my Savior, whose presence in my life inspires the words that I pen to paper. Second, I thank my father, Sgt. John Scott Smith, US Army Korea, for the poems he wrote in a foxhole during battle. My family found these poems in a box under his bed after his death. Treasures he kept private from his family I now share in this book. Thank you, Dad!

Contents

Acknowledgments

Thanks to my good friend Janelle Sheldon for helping to type and organize my poems into book form.

Hello, God

Look, God, I have never spoken to You,
But now I want to say, "How do You do?"
You see, God, they told me You didn't exist,
and like a fool, I believed all this.

Last night, from a shell hole, I saw Your sky—
I figured right then they had told me a lie.
Had I taken time to see things You made,
I'd have known they weren't calling a spade a spade.

I wonder, God, if You'd shake my hand;
somehow I feel that You will understand.
Funny, I had to come to this hellish place
before I had time to see Your face.

Well, I guess there isn't much more to say,
but I'm sure glad, God, I met You today.
I guess the *zero hour* will soon be here,
but I'm not afraid, since I know You're near.

The signal! Well, God, I'll have to go;
I like You lots, this I want You to know.
Look now, this will be a horrible fight—
who knows, I may come to Your house tonight.

Though I wasn't friendly to You before,
I wonder, God, if You'd wait at Your door.
Look I'm crying! Me! Shedding these tears,
I wish I had known You these many years.

Well, I have to go now, God. Goodbye!
Strange, since I met You, I'm not afraid to die.

Sgt. John S. Smith

Korea

Just below the Manchurian border
Kumwha is the spot
Where we are doomed to spend our time
In the land that God forgot

Down with the snakes and lizards
Where the mud is thick as glue
Right in the middle of nowhere
Ten thousand miles from you

We sweat, we freeze, we shiver
It's more than a man can stand
We're not supposed to be convicts
Just defenders of our land

We're soldiers of the Seventh Division
Earning a measly pay
Guarding people with millions
For only $2.40 a day

Living with our memories
Waiting to see our babies
Hoping that while we're away
That they haven't married yet

Nobody knows we're living
Nobody gives a damn
At home, we mustn't be forgotten
We belong to Uncle Sam

Sgt. John S. Smith

America

A Cowboy's Prayer

When I no longer ride tall in the saddle,
give me the grace to keep fighting this battle.
The image in the mirror seems a different man.
I draw comfort from each day spent on the ranch.

When I feel my strength growing weaker,
may I look to Jesus, my teacher.
To give thanks for every day my boots go on,
and sit on the back porch in the sun.

For someday I'll kick off these boots
and retire them for sandal shoes.
At that time, my chores will be done.
I'll be walking home with Jesus, God's Son.

A Nation Cries

A young gunman fires, indifference paints his face.
He aims, shoots down thirty-two classmates.
Gunfire echoes through the halls of the Virginia Tech campus.
Students run—confused, frightened, in anguish.

Methodically he goes from room to room,
Leaving death, destruction—a thick cloud of doom.
He chains the doors to prevent escape—
makes himself arbiter of his fellow students' fates.

A sense of disbelief spreads across our land.
This devastating news has us questioning God's plan.
Our nation is under attack!
We've watched our beliefs, our morals, veer off track.

We've shut out God from our government, homes, and schools.
We've trampled God's Ten Commandments and His "Golden Rule."
When will we recall our nation's cornerstone,
allowing God to lead us in government, schools, and homes?

When will we as a people cry, "We have had enough!"?
We, as a Christian nation, call out, "We want God with us!"
This is no time to keep secret all that God can do,
for He can heal this nation, when we let His Son shine through.

Cries of Our Forefathers

America— "In God we've put our trust."
Freedom paid for by those who fought for us.
A nation that once allowed prayer in school,
where children learned the Golden Rule.

Now violence is prevalent over our land.
People are afraid to take a stand.
We no longer have respect for ourselves,
so hence, we have no respect for anyone else.

Prayer in school is no longer allowed.
Shootings and hatred are common—our children lash out.
When will we learn freedom can be abused,
when no one has to follow any rules.

The answer is still to put our trust in God.
America's people need guidance from above.
Prayer in school, work, and play
should be the start of everyone's day!

Let us learn from our Forefathers long ago;
"America needs God" their cry on the wind blows.
Freedom is everyone's responsibility.
Our God reigns from "sea to shining sea."

The Lamb in School

Another child was shot today
by a child who was led astray.
The senseless killing of our children in schools
defiantly breaks all of God's rules.

I place my child in God's care,
each time I send her into the world—out there.
I pray she will return unharmed,
knowing she's in God's arms.

It is time we allow the Lamb of God
back into school, to show His love.
So the senseless killing will be the past,
and children can safely go to class.

Wake-Up Call

America is under attack:
The World Trade Center's twin towers explode and collapse.
Hundreds of Americans buried in rubble;
securities of our nation bursting like a bubble.

Four hijacked planes used as bombs,
the third flies into the Pentagon.
The center of our nation's military
on fire, leaving people injured and buried.

A fourth plane explodes into the ground,
in a field, away from any towns.
Americans on the plane had taken a stand.
As heroes, they took matters into their own hands.

America's people can't believe it's true
as they watch or listen to the horrific news.
This only happens across the sea!
How can this be happening in our own country?

This is a wake-up call to the land of Democracy:
that God is needed to keep this land free.
A nation that was built on her forefathers' faith
needs God back in government, schools, and in each state.

Christmas

Born a King

Some believe that the Christ Child is a fable.
How could a King be born in a stable?
The Son of God, born of the Virgin Mary!
It seems as unreal as believing in fairies.

In my heart, I know that this Christ Child is real.
My faith and His grace make life easier to deal.
The light of the world was born that night,
in a Bethlehem stable, under a star so bright.

Prophets foretold of this wondrous story,
when this miracle child would bring heaven's glory.
This child, the King that brought life anew:
Baby Jesus, a Savior, the King of the Jews.

For those who doubt this Christmas story,
my heart aches and for them I am sorry.
A Savior, a King, comes this Christmas.
May we open our hearts and let Him live in us.

Fear Not

"Fear not, I bring you good news!"
to eliminate those Christmas blues.
Christmas cards, shopping, and wrapping seems endless;
where is the money needed? We haven't a guess!

It's time to stop this holiday bustle.
It's time to slow down our daily hustle.
To celebrate Jesus is the reason,
for this holiday season.

Like shepherds a long time ago,
let us run to the manger, with our heads bowed low.
Let this Christmas truly mean
that the Christ Child is born in you and me.

First Christmas Morn

Joseph's dream fulfilled what prophets foretold:
that Mary, a virgin, a Son she would hold.
A Son conceived in her from God above,
Jesus, the name they would give this Son of love.

Joseph awoke, did what the angel commanded:
upheld the responsibilities that God had handed.
He was to take Mary as his new wife.
And together, they would begin a new life.

A census from Caesar Augustus sent them to the town of David.
In a town called Bethlehem, Mary bore our Savior.
Wrapped in cloths, placed in a manger, as there was no room at the
    inn,
a humbled birthplace was provided for the Savior who came to save
    us from sin.

Angels, shepherds, and kings came to marvel at the blessed Child,
and Mary treasured all these things, and tenderly smiled.
With the quiet neigh of a donkey and the soft bleating of sheep,
the beloved Christ Child was rocked to sleep.

That first Christmas morn our Savior came
to bring healing to all, even the blind and the lame.
What a glorious sight it is to look upon the Christ Child's face,
a Child who brought this world His saving grace.

God's Gift

The coming of the Messiah has long been foretold
through generations by prophets of old.
A virgin was to give birth
to the Messiah, the Savior of the earth.

Born in a Bethlehem stable stall,
a gift from God to one and all.
God's gift of love, sent to make us all one,
His plan sent to earth as Mary's newborn son.

To those who have long waited for this Child King,
new meaning and hope He now brings.
A gift from the Father in heaven above,
whose wondrous Gift was born out of His love.

May God bless you this Christmas season, as we remember the Christ
    Child.

In a Manger

Joseph took Mary across the desert sand,
on a small donkey, to a town called Bethlehem.
Mary was expecting her firstborn son—
a gift from God, the Anointed One.

The town was crowded, there was no room at the inn.
In a manger, our Savior was born—He came to take away sin.
Sent by an angel, the shepherds journeyed to see
the small child who would change history.

Wise men from the east, came from afar
to gaze upon the Christ child, sleeping under the bright star.
Gifts of gold, frankincense, and myrrh they brought,
as they found, in a manger, the King they sought.

In that manger, Christ we come to see,
as we celebrate His birth on bended knee.
Let us look upon Christmas with a new joy,
for God has given, to us, this precious baby boy.

What Shall I Bring?

What gift do I bring to the Baby wrapped in swaddling clothes?
For I do not own myrrh, frankincense, or gold.
What present do I bring to the Child in the manger?
How about kindness to a stranger?

What do I say to my Lord in the manger?
That I forgive the one whom has caused me anger.
As I kneel and pray to Baby Jesus,
I know that through Him, there is forgiveness.

What gift do I bring to the Christ Child, my Lord and King?
What can I offer, what can I bring?
He smiles and reaches up to me.
I will show His love for all to see.

Easter

Blessed Assurance

Mocked and scorned, beaten 'til near death.
The cries of "Crucify Him!" were heard above the rest.
Pilate tried to wash his hands of the conviction—
he did not know what to do with Jesus, he did not understand Him.

For Pilate could not have known that he could not change God's
    plan,
that it was Jesus's destiny to be the Lamb for all men.
Hung on a cross with two thieves on each side,
Jesus suffered, cried "It's finished," put His head down, and died.

The women, watching and weeping, took him down to be buried.
Was this the end of the Son of Mary?
Was mankind left with the heartache: "It should have been us in His
    place"?
Wasn't He supposed to save the human race?

For three days, His disciples hid and stumbled about.
Their leader was gone—no one could figure it out.
Are we like Pilate, ready to wash our hands?
Are we running and hiding from God's greater plan?

Up from the grave Jesus arose,
with a mighty victory over all His foes!
Good News that brings blessed assurance,
that death did not keep Christ from us.

Help us always to remember that first Easter morn.
Let us shout and blow the loud trumpet horn!
Our Lord is alive—He has cheated death!
All who believe in Him, He will truly bless.

Love on a Cross

On a hillside, called Calvary,
three crosses stood, for all to see.
Three men were hung for crimes committed,
One should have been acquitted.

Jesus hung there, tried and convicted,
just as prophets of old had predicted.
Christ the Messiah would come to save,
Death could not silence Him or hold Him in the grave.

Love hung on the cross that Easter morn,
forgiveness to all—new life was born!
So as I look to the cross, my life is forgiven.
My Savior, my Lord, from death He is risen!

Mighty King

A King accused, beaten, and scorned.
A mere man, His visage forlorn.
A crown of thorns, rested atop His head.
His back, stripped of flesh, whipped 'til it bled.

He stood in front of the angry crowd,
until cries of "Crucify Him!" grew loud.
They forced Him to carry His cross.
His popularity with His people was lost.

Nails were driven in His hands and feet;
a promise of salvation He came to keep.
"King of the Jews" the sign above Him said.
"Forgive them," He whispered, and bowed His head.

Could this be our mighty King?
The voices of denial loudly ring.
He's quiet now, He's near death.
He fought the fight, He gave His best.

There is a happy ending ahead,
for Christ resurrected from the dead.
The cross did not end this man's life—
salvation for everyone He bought that night!

One Dark Night

The world went dark, and there came a mother's cry.
Mary knelt at the cross, watching her son die.
Hours before, an angry crowd yelled, "Crucify Him!"
Little did they know, it was all a plan to save us from sin.

Kneeling with Jesus's mother were Mary, Mary Magdalene, and His
    beloved disciple, John,
to whom Jesus said, "Behold your mother, mother behold your son."
Even with dying breath, Jesus took care of those He loved.
"It is finished!" He cried, and He looked to his Father above.

The tomb was dark—they sealed it with a large stone.
All who knew Jesus were lost and alone.
Arriving to care for His body, Mary Magdalene saw the stone rolled
    away.
"They have taken our Lord!" were the only words she could say.

Peter and another ran to the tomb to see.
The disciple who was there first entered, he saw and believed.
Crying outside the tomb, Mary saw two men.
"They have taken my Lord, and I don't know where they put Him!"

She turned to leave and saw another man standing there.
Not knowing her Lord, she still wept in despair.
"Who are you looking for?" Jesus said.
In that moment, Mary recognized her Lord, who had risen from the
    dead!

Jesus's promise was fulfilled, His death a payment for the world's sin,
for all who believe and live their lives through Him.
God's plan was complete, the prophecies came true.
In Christ Jesus, your sins are forgiven, your life is made new!

This Easter

As the lily blooms in spring,
new life this Easter brings.
Washed away are all my sins.
As Jesus dies, new life begins.

Closer to Jesus I want to feel.
So before the cross, I must kneel.
New joy overflows my heart.
Healing begins as from my sins I part.

Easter is not a time of sorrow,
but hope, through Jesus, for a new tomorrow;
as I turn to look at Jesus' face,
and forever know His saving grace.

Through Mary's Eyes

My son, Jesus, hung from a tree
for all of Jerusalem to see.
Soldiers mocked Him and crowned Him with thorns,
they gambled for the clothes that He had worn.

I stood and watched Him die.
I listened to His final cries.
He said, "Woman, behold your son!"
At death He cried, "It is finished, God's work is done."

My heart was heavy with gloom.
We placed His body in a tomb.
Lying there, He was now at peace,
away from the people He was sent to set free.

Death of a child: a mother's worst fear.
I prayed, "God, help me!" through my tears.
A grief that seemed like it would never end,
my son is gone, the Son God sent.

I went to His tomb; it was empty and bare.
I heard someone cry, "Jesus is no longer here!"
Death's grip, my Son had overcome.
Final victory He claimed, eternal life He won.

Walk to Calvary

As I take a walk out to Calvary,
God's love is there for all to see.
Jesus hangs on a cross to fulfill a promise.
Through Him, new life is given to us.

Here on Calvary, I look to the cross,
where Christ hangs for the suffering and the lost.
For it was God who held Jesus's hands and feet steady,
to bring redemption to those who are open and ready.

His Holy blood spilled on the ground,
as the night turned silent and darkness fell around.
"Forgive them," He gasped—it was His last prayer.
Silence was broken, and all became aware.

Without hesitation, He gave his life so I would believe
in a Savior on a cross, on a hill called Calvary.

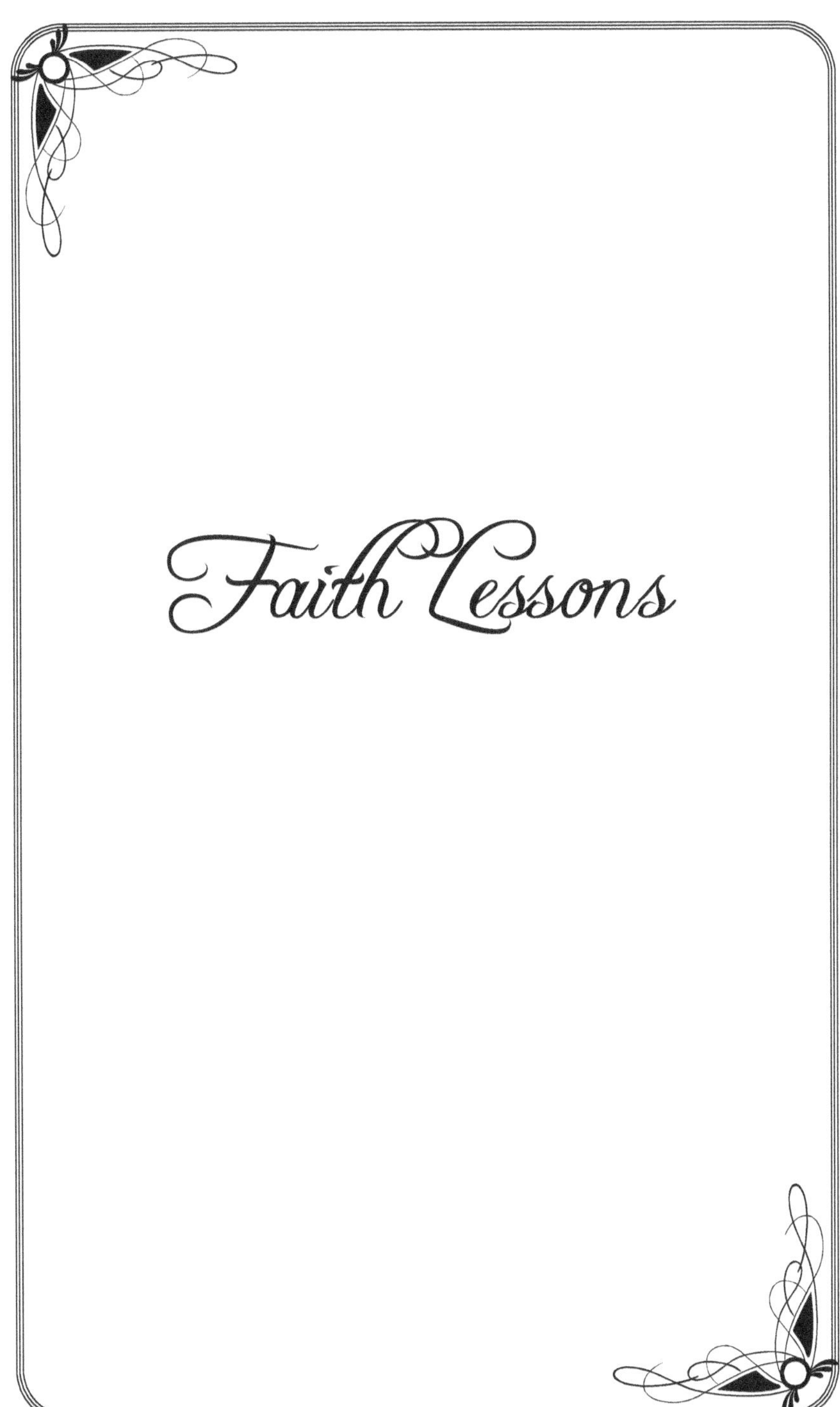

Faith Lessons

A Light in Darkness

I feel the whole world is against me.
Darkness is all around, so I can't see.
Anger has led me out of control;
the devil is master of my soul.

My behavior is influenced by my choice in friends.
They say they're with me 'til the end.
Is this the road I must go?
Please, help me to say, "No."

Where are all my friends right now?
As I sit alone in the darkness, with my head bowed,
a still small voice answers, "I am here!
I will not leave you, do not fear."

In the room of darkness, there is a light—
His name is Jesus. He's helping me tonight.
My darkened heart has been made whole,
my Lord Jesus is taking back my soul.

By His Grace

Life is a fleeting moment in time.
The Lord has given us a sign,
that by His unending grace,
we can stop this rapid pace.

So when you're in a big rush,
take a second and listen for the hush
of the wind blowing through the leaves,
or the birds singing in the trees.

For each of us is given
a chance for peaceful living.
It is by our Lord's grace
we will survive and live in this place.

Environments

Different environments are part of us.
This is why in God we must put our trust.
Please, Lord, help us to shine our light
no matter what our plight.

For Christ is in everyone;
it's up to us to show the Son.
With God as our guide,
His light we will not hide.

Go out into the world and shine
so those who see will no longer be blind.
Let Christ rule our environments
so everyone will know through God we are sent.

Extraordinary Love

It's hard to understand
that forgiveness is part of God's plan.
God possesses an extraordinary love,
for even a sinner is loved from above.

God is searching for the lost.
He will not give up, no matter the cost.
Even those far from God
will not be without His love.

For hate may be strong,
but God's love will right the wrong.
God's love is yours to gain.
His love will heal all your pain.

Facing the Unknown

When life is going great,
bad news comes—there must be a mistake.
After all, you've been feeling fine,
so this news is blowing your mind.

Until there is a trial in life we must face,
we feel comfortable and safe.
So why does this happen right now?
There are fields to tend and plow.

God's answers to our questions seem nonexistent.
What we need is the patience to listen.
Give the problem to Him, for His love is true.
God's love and healing will see you through.

Forgiveness

Often, in the course of one's life,
someone we know causes us strife.
We get angry and will not forgive.
Do you think that is what *Jesus* did?

So let us put our differences aside,
and forgive the past mistakes and abide
in what *Jesus* tried to teach us—
to have love and forgiveness.

That someday with forgiveness
we will learn to live with *Jesus* in us.
So if we are wronged by a friend,
forgiveness is what we seek in the end.

Hiding

How many times in life
have I denied Christ?
Just like Peter who turned his face,
I run to hide from God's grace.

Has the rooster crowed for me today?
When confronted, will I know what to say?
I sometimes choose to look on from afar,
instead of following that bright star.

I try to run and hide from Christ;
I can never be out of His sight.
For His love and forgiveness is always there;
I just need to ask for them in prayer.

In This World

Wake up and get ready to go!
Eat my breakfast and watch the morning news show.
Frustration and anxiety set in with all the bad news.
Feeling overwhelmed with not knowing what to do.

Jesus told us we would be strangers in this land.
We may feel like we are drowning in quicksand.
Don't lose heart, as Jesus has come to conquer it all!
Victory is His—He will not fall!

So cast away all that doubt and fear.
Get on your knees, pray—His arms are near.
Lean in and feel His comfort and grace.
Go live in this world and show Christ's face.

Leap of Faith

When do I know to take a leap?
To learn to stand on my own two feet?
It's easier to rely on someone else,
than to have faith in myself.

It is always easier to play it safe,
but maybe I should trust in God's grace.
For only a leap will set me free,
and help me become what I want to be.

So, please, dear Lord, take my hand,
and let me know this is part of Your plan.
When I learn to trust You first,
my fears, like balloons, all will burst.

My Sharp Tongue!

Sometimes I wish I lived in a bubble,
where my sharp tongue would cause no trouble.
A gift from God is my tongue and voice;
to use them to speak softly and make right choices.

A gift, when used wrong, causes so much pain,
when we turn and speak to someone in vain.
Speaking words in frustration and anger
to someone we know, or a stranger.

Is this how I should use this gift?
My voice in praise I should lift!
In prayer, I can ask God above
to right my wrongs with His love.

Not Just a Vacation!

God wants to be more than a vacation spot.
Involved in your life, more than a dot.
Like the wind, He is always there,
but we do not notice 'til we need comfort from fear.

God wants to be more than a weekend getaway.
He wants to be your home, not just in town on a brief stay.
God is a dwelling place!
Under His roof, there is amazing grace.

Not just a one-night stand.
He is the Rock for which we forever will stand.
He wants to be the one in whom we live.
To Him all of our life we must give.

Not Now, Lord!

Like an excited child, running on ahead,
not listening to what her Father has said.
Running and making her own choice,
ignoring her Father's heavenly voice.

Not taking time to listen for His answer,
jumping around, like a crazed dancer.
Not reaching for His outstretched hand
as he leads me through His laid-out plan.

I sit and pout, like a small child,
my life around me has grown wild.
Putting the blame on someone else,
instead of looking inward, toward myself.

I sit down and start to cry,
realizing the problem is I.
My Father calls my name, loud and clear,
saying, "I forgive you!" and wipes my tears.

One Day

One day…there will be no one in need.
One day…there will be no one to feed.
One day…there will be no guns or war.
One day…there will be peace from shore to shore.

One day…there will be no hate.
One day…there will be nothing to debate.
One day…there will be no one alone.
One day…everyone will have a home.

One day…our Lord will come down
to take a big look around.
One day…there will be no more wait,
for the Lord will take us to heaven's gate.

He will ask if you're ready one day.
What are you going to say?
The day will soon be here.
Today is the time to prepare.

Perfection

In this world we expect perfection.
We look to find it in our own reflection.
Falling short of the goal,
we see failure and feel out of control.

Perfection became man at Jesus's birth.
He forgives our failures and shows us our worth.
God became man to lead us down the right road.
He embraces our burden, He lightens our load.

Jesus graciously suffered, died, and rose so we could live,
asking only of us our hearts to Him we give.
Trusting and showing the world God's light,
to God is the glory, using His wisdom and insight.

As I pray on bended knee to my Lord above,
I ask for Him to use me to show the world His love.
Show me and lead me as part of Your plan,
You are my rock, Lord, on which I stand.

Seeing Clearly

Sometimes it's hard to understand
what is in God's plan.
Sometimes it takes a second time
before we see, like the man who was blind.

Spiritual truth is not always perceived
as we would like it to be.
The answers may not be clear, like ink on a page;
Jesus may choose to show us in stages.

What we need is a little trust
that Christ in His time will show us.
The message we really need
will be brought to light so we can see.

Slaying a Giant

Off in a foreign land,
across the desert sand.
In a time long ago,
the fear of a giant on the wind blows.

A champion of the Philistines was he.
Goliath stood for all to see.
He wore armor from head to toe.
No one could defeat this foe.

The Israelites were to send one man
to fight this giant, hand to hand.
David said, "Don't lose heart, I will go,
for my God will deliver me—this I know."

Goliath laughed with joy,
for the Israelites had sent a boy.
But David was not afraid.
He reached for the stone in his bag.

He threw it and struck Goliath's head.
The Philistines' giant now was dead.
The men of Israel began to shout,
their enemy ran all about.

A mere boy this victory won,
for he was God's chosen one.
David slayed a giant that day,
because he trusted what God had to say.

The Lord Rejoices When We Sing!

The Lord rejoices when we sing.
It is with our voices our praises we bring.
We may not feel worthy of this test.
But a song that's sung freely is always the best.

Praising Him is always your choice,
so let us praise Him with a loud voice.
Let a joyful song fill the air,
even off-key—the Lord does not care!

Let the world hear you rejoice.
Let the Lord hear your voice.
For everyone should hear the Lord is King!
Let us rejoice and praise Him as we sing!

To Touch a Life

I often think of my life here on earth.
Have I given it all that I'm worth?
To have confidence that my life has touched someone,
so I may be encouraged to fight 'til the victory is won.

For we are all given but one life,
to make it the best in the midst of strife.
We all are influenced by someone else.
So let me touch a life myself.

When people think of me,
do they see what I see?
Do they see me as giving it my all,
without fear of taking a fall?

I pray my life will inspire
to believe in someone much higher.
I sometimes wonder where to begin.
First, my life I must entrust to Him.

Trials of Life

The road of life is winding,
with every turn somewhat blinding.
The only way to survive
is to have Jesus by your side.

If life gives you a wrong turn,
and you feel like you've been burned,
just bow your head in prayer,
and know your Lord is there.

They say God only gives us
problems we can handle.
I say just walk…
with the Man in the sandals.

The problem will go away.
The sun will shine on a new day.
With each new trial of life,
some relief from the strife.

Let Jesus walk with you,
For only He can see you through.

Waiting for an Answer

All is quiet, except for the clock ticking.
The one movement is the cat's tail, twitching.
It's at these times I lay and wait
for the answer to the problem I put on God's plate.

Sometimes the answer comes.
Other times, I get up and reach for my Tums.
For I must learn it is not my time.
For God's time is the reason for this rhyme.

So now I lay back down to sleep,
asking the Lord my soul to keep.
Praying, please, Lord, give me patience tonight,
and wait 'til tomorrow for your insight.

Family

A Mother's Prayer

A child conceived by our love,
a gift from God, in heaven above.
A blessing bestowed on your father and I,
as we look forward to hearing your first cry.

Soon you'll learn to crawl, walk, and run.
Memories I'll cherish to remember the fun.
I'll be there to help with all of life's test,
but I know you'll give it your very best.

Life's road may turn good to bad.
Your emotions may go from happy to sad.
"My love will comfort you" is my prayer,
but always know Jesus will be there.

Father

You're there to pick me up when I fall.
You cheered from the sidelines as I gave it my all.
You taught me how to ride a bike.
You taught me about the woods on family hikes.

When fishing, hunting, or camping, you showed me the ropes.
You gave me life lessons, making it easier to cope.
Like "When life throws you a sudden curve,
you must hang on tight and try to swerve."

Sometimes life may turn upside down.
Your being there keeps my feet on the ground.
You always show me unconditional love,
and continue to pray for me, to our Lord up above.

You've always been there to lend a hand—
teaching me, helping me to understand.
Your belief in God, country, and family is true,
and there are no greater colors than red, white, and blue.

For you've fought to keep us free and safe,
to fully rely on God's grace,
that all things are possible if you trust in God above,
and there is no greater thing than a Father's love.

Thank you, Dad, for always being there,
for loving and showing that you always care.
For I know I can face any of life's tests,
because I have been taught by the very best!

Into This World, a Child

My life is so blessed; I begin to sing,
of new life to this world that I will bring.
My baby inside my womb continues to grow;
I feel the kicking of those little toes.

After years of praying to my Lord above,
a baby He's given, for me to love.
I pray for continued health for us,
for in His hands, I put my trust.

Let me be a good parent, like my Father above,
showing my child unconditional love.
Continue, Lord, to help and teach us
so my child, too, will walk with Jesus.

My Love for You

As long as I can remember, you've been part of my life.
I cherish the day we became husband and wife.
Our paths were destined to join as one.
I thank God your love I have won.

There will be times that are good and bad.
There will be memories that make us happy and sad.
I know that with you by my side,
we'll be able to endure this ride.

Love, when nurtured, grows like ripples in the pond—
a love that you can always count on.
I pray our love will grow this way,
for by your side, I intend to stay.

In an instant I would say, again, the words "I do,"
for I know our Lord is there to see us through.
So when I become impatient and unglued,
find comfort in knowing I'll always love you.

My Mother

The stories that you once told
are becoming true, as I grow old.
Like "Time flies the older you get!"
or "You'll have a child just like you, I bet!"

But one thing I can honestly say,
is that without you, Mom, I wouldn't be here today.
A wonderful role model you are to me,
which has made me the woman I came to be.

You taught me how to set my priorities straight,
like "There's nothing worse than being late!"
To God, family, and my country I am true,
because I've grown up watching you.

So this poem is my tribute to you,
for you've touched my life in all you do.
My life has truly been blessed
to have been loved by a mother who is the best.

Friendship

A Different Road

A different direction in life you must go,
as you head down a different road.
Best wishes and love to you, my friend.
Goodbye for now, our friendship will not end.

Friendships are a gift from God, above;
friendships that are blessed with His love.
Remember as you leave from here,
you are loved by your peers.

I know you have made a good choice,
but please call, if you need a friendly voice.
In life, we are blessed by those we meet,
your smile and friendship, in my heart, I'll keep.

Be a Friend

(To the chorus of "Friends" by Michael W. Smith)

Be a friend forever,
lead them to the Lord.
Don't ever say, "Never,"
'cause Christ is your Lord.

Don't talk, take action,
with God as your guide.
For a lifetime's not too long
to live for Christ.

Friendship

A friendship that warms my heart;
it helps me on days with a rough start.
Life is better because I know you.
Your kindness helps to see me through.

Days that seemed like they'd never end
were better because of you, my friend.
So as you head down a different road,
just call—I'll be there to lighten your load.

Friendships are bound in love,
strengthened by our Lord, above.
Friendships built by Christ are forever;
friendships that make our lives better.

God Gave Me You

When I was without a friend,
God gave me you.
When I needed a hug or smile,
you knew what to do.

I think of you often in the week.
I know God crossed our paths for us to meet.
A friendship that has sustained me through tough times,
a feeling of love no matter what's on the line.

I thank God each and every day
that our friendship is here to stay.
We know not what may lay ahead,
our friendship is here without a word said.

One Small Church

One small church
can heal the hurt
of one lonely soul
who's lost and out of control.

When I walked in,
I became one of them.
Their arms open wide,
they took me inside.

My heart has been changed,
my life rearranged.
To follow Christ is my goal.
Thank You, Lord, for saving my soul.

One small church
has ended my search.
A family I have found,
and a love that holds no bounds.

To the Movies

There's a movie I'd like to see.
Would you, my friend, go with me?
As we sit to visit and rest,
analyzing the movie, putting it to our test.

There is nowhere else I'd rather be
than to the movies, just you and me.
For a few hours of the day,
we escape this world and get away.

It doesn't matter what the feature,
a drama, comedy, or alien space creature,
with a soda and popcorn in hand,
going to the movies is always a plan!

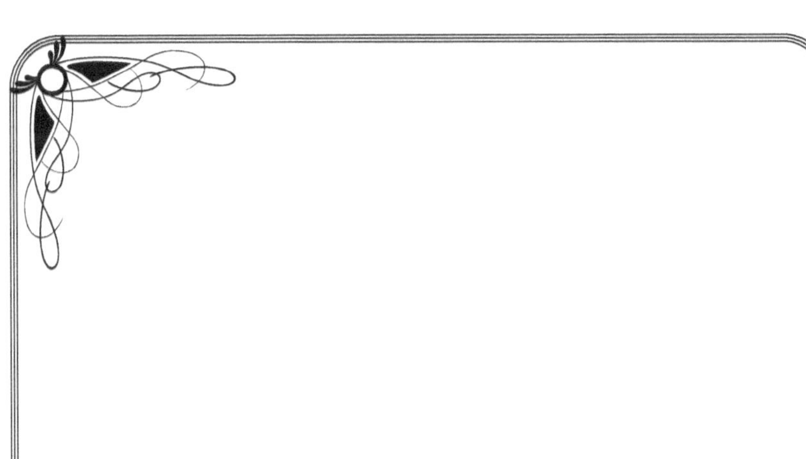

Jesus, My Savior

A Walk on Water

In the midst of a storm,
a small fishing boat looked forlorn.
The boat, like a toy used in play,
was tossed in the wind and spray.

Out across the water, Jesus came.
The fishermen, not knowing His name—
as this "Ghost" drew near,
they cried out in fear.

Jesus said, "Fear not, it is I!
I will not let you die."
Peter called, "If it is really true,
let me walk on water to you."

The Lord said, "Alright, come along."
Peter stepped out, feeling quite strong.
But as he looked at the high waves,
he started to sink, crying to be saved.

The Lord Jesus took Peter's hand,
for Peter's rescue was part of his plan.
"O man of little faith," Jesus said,
"After all I've taught and led,
you still continue to doubt Me.
When will you begin to see?"
The storm stopped, the waves grew calm.
Peter's doubt left him frightened and wrong.

Arms Open Wide

All the miracles that Peter witnessed seemed like a dream,
for he was accused of being seen with this crucified King.
As one of Jesus's chosen twelve, he denied Him three times,
even after sharing the last supper of bread and wine.

An act of betrayal was a kiss on Jesus's cheek,
as Judas' temptation of money left him vulnerable and weak.
In his shame he could not go on,
so he hanged himself for what he did to God's Son.

For neither man could know it was all part of God's plan.
They could not understand their love for this man.
Even betrayed and denied, Christ's love did not waver.
He was born to die, the world's Messiah and Savior.

He showed His love with His arms opened wide.
It was that love that held Him on the cross to die.
The act of love that sealed his fate:
with His own blood, He cleansed a believer's slate.

Come, Follow Me

Come, follow Me, Jesus said.
On the cross, for you, I died and bled.
Salvation is yours, this gift is free.
All you need is faith to come follow Me.

The gift I give brings eternal rewards.
After this life, I wait for you at heaven's door.
So follow Me, do not worry, I will take the lead.
I will not run ahead but go at your speed.

I have walked this path to show you the way.
I will be beside you every day.
So do not be anxious or live in fear,
you will feel My presence, as I am always near.

So take up your own cross and follow Me.
Cast your nets into the world's sea.
Be a light to those around you.
Soon they too will come follow Me.

Just One Touch

A large crowd gathered around.
The word of His miracles spread through the town.
They say this man is someone special.
If I could just get close enough to touch a tassel!

Just one touch of the hem of His robe,
healing from my affliction He would bestow.
I believe this healer is the One,
Teacher, Rabbi, Messiah, Jesus, God's Son.

Closer, closer, almost there!
A reach, a touch, if I dare…
A break in the crowd, now is my chance!
He turns toward me, love in His glance.

"Who touched Me?" Jesus said.
I sunk to the ground and bowed my head.
He knelt to look into my eyes,
"Your faith has healed you, My child!"

Just one touch changed my life!
My body made whole, my life made right.

My Life, For You

My life for you I dedicate.
New life for you beyond heaven's gate.
I hung on the cross, beaten and scorned,
but rose for you on Easter morn.

For I am the Son of the Creator,
sent down to earth to save God's people.
Blessed are those who truly believe,
who have faith before they can see.

I ask of you only one thing:
your life to Me you gladly bring.
For when you're tired and blue,
remember *I lived my life for you.*

One Man

A long time ago, God sent His Son
to die on the cross for everyone.
This One Man showed His love for us.
This One Man had *the right stuff.*

He may have been born in a stable,
but this great Man was very able
to rise up out of a world of sin.
All who know Him, a new life begin.

For God's only Son
would give Himself for everyone,
to show us what we really need
is faith as great as a little seed.

Walking with My King

I skip to the beat
as I walk along the street.
My heart begins to sing
when I walk with my king.

Taking the time to talk
to my Lord as I walk,
I give thanks for all the love
from heaven up above.

For everyone is blessed
with His righteousness.
Everyone has a home;
in Him, we are not alone.

So take the time today
to give thanks and to pray.
Your life you may bring
when you walk with the King.

Loss, Loneliness, and Grieving

A Child Cries

A small child cries in the corner, afraid to let someone hear.
They can never get used to the beatings or living in fear.
In the news, another parent is arrested for the death of a child.
We question how anyone can raise a hand to something so small and
      mild.

Where is God? Does He not hear His small children crying?
How is it their parents are the cause of their dying?
These are hard questions for a society rampant with crime!
Is this just another sign for the end of times?

Jesus is there, in the dark corner, with His arms around the small
      child.
He is aware that this child's parents are mad and have turned wild.
Jesus took the beatings and was left to die.
He hung on the cross—"It is finished," He cried.

As we read the child's story, we are saddened with the news.
We have to remember the child will be safe with the "King of the
      Jews."
The child is now free from this life and runs to their true Father's
      arms,
where They know that there is no one to cause them any harm.

A Prayer for Comfort

I look around for a sign,
an answer to my prayer.
Give me comfort, Lord,
to know You're with me here.

Help me not to walk alone,
but to accept Your outstretched hand.
Lead me on this troubled path,
carry me through the sinking sand.

So on these lonely nights
let me feel Your presence—near.
Keep me close to You.
Help me with my fear.

Alone

Sitting all alone.
Waiting for a call on the phone.
Wondering if anyone out there
will take the time to care.

A card, a letter in the mail,
would help the loneliness sail
away from your mind for awhile,
and add to your face a smile.

If this feeling comes your way,
there is someone who'll listen every day.
He is always there for you;
the only friend who can be true.

All that you need today
is an open heart, able to pray.
Jesus is always there to heal
the loneliness that you feel.

Comfort in a Storm

There will always be stormy weather.
In God's arms, you're like a feather;
cradled like a small child,
as the storm around you grows strong and wild.

Calmness comes through prayer;
giving God your troubles and cares.
Facing the storm, with God at your side,
knowing you don't have to run and hide.

Run and cry in His strong arms,
find comfort and safety from harm.
Let yourself be carried across the sand.
Remember your life is in God's hands.

So when your life takes a turn for the worst,
look toward heaven—put God first.
When stormy winds tear at your sail,
God is with you—His love will not fail.

Goodbye for Now

As I walk through the valley of death,
I'll walk toward my Lord for final rest.
All I need is to touch His face,
to feel His awesome presence and grace.

Although it will be tough to leave the ones I love,
Peace surrounds me, for I'm in His arms of love.
A love that has carried me on this road.
A love that has lightened my heavy load.

Don't cry now, try to be strong.
Look for comfort in my Lord's arms.
Reach out to those who love you.
Ask Jesus to help you through.

For now, I've walked my final mile—
my Lord is there with a loving smile.
Remember goodbye will not be forever.
Someday, we'll again be together.

Hope

"My *hope* is built on nothing less
than Jesus's blood and righteousness."
Words to a hymn that is held dear
to help comfort lives filled with fear.

For our *hope* is in our Lord, Jesus.
He is always there with us.
We are in His everlasting arms.
He gives us comfort, He keeps us from harm.

Help us, Lord, to find comfort in You.
No matter what we face, You'll see us through!
When our earthly body begins to tire,
He leads us to Him as we expire.

Our *hope* is built on our Creator in heaven above.
In Him there is faith, *hope*, and love.

In His Arms

Into His arms she is running,
For her death was fast in coming.
Her life here on earth was cut short.
Heaven is her final port.

As we lay awake wondering, *Why not I?*
we must turn to His arms when we cry.
For those of us still here
will draw strength from others we hold dear.

We are not promised life without pain.
Comfort we find in Christ's holy flame.
For His light is strong for us to see,
as we walk on earth, 'til we meet again in eternity.

In His Hands

In His hands, He hears you cry.
In His hands, He wipes your eyes.
In His hands, He holds you as you tremble and shake.
In His hands, He is with you while you're awake.

Comfort is there for you, in His hands.
He holds you up, through the pain, while you try to stand.
He cries tears of happiness and joy with you,
giving you comfort with everything you must go through.

Remember in this life you are not alone.
Love blooms—everywhere the seeds you've sown have grown.
Lean on family and friends, who love you.
In His hands, let Him carry you in all you do.

Losing My Job

I was told at work today,
"The company is downsizing"—I start unemployment pay.
I'm an out-of-work medical lab technician.
Finding a job? I'll have to be a magician!

The first few months were like a vacation.
After a hard year, I deserve a little relaxation.
Spending more time with family and friends,
I was hoping the fun never ends.

Realizing I would need to work soon,
I sent resumes to everyone, except those on the moon!
I got a chance at a few interviews.
Nothing worked out, now what do I do?

I must set my mind to try harder,
to set my goals just a little farther.
I'm learning to trust God's timing,
for He will send me a job worth finding.

So as I sit and write this poem,
give me strength, dear Lord, to keep going.
For I know I will land on my feet,
and my needs, my Lord, You will always meet.

Never Alone

Do not be discouraged, for Jesus is near.
When He sees you crying, He'll wipe your tears.
The road ahead may seem long.
Lean on Jesus, and you'll be strong.

From your side He will never leave.
When you're troubled, He also grieves.
It is Jesus that is holding your hand,
when you feel like you're in sinking sand.

Don't be afraid to lean on those who love you.
They are in your life to help you through.
Our loved ones are our greatest gifts from above.
Through them we see and feel God's love.

Never alone, you're never alone.
God is with you always, you're never alone.

One Year Later

It's been a year since we said goodbye…
The thought still brings tears to my eyes.
As I stare into the cold, wintry sky above,
warmth from heaven comes to me, from your love.
For we will see each other again,
when the road I travel comes to an end.

Seek His Arms

The world is yours—life is going great!
Bad news comes, you cry, "It's a mistake!"
After all, you're young and feeling fine.
So this can't be happening—it's a dream in your mind.

There are trials that are unfair but must be faced.
They leave you feeling vulnerable and unsafe.
You're confused, asking the question, "What did I do?"
Seek His arms to hold you, heal you, and see you through.

God's answers may seem slow, even nonexistent.
Take time to be still, patient, quiet, and listen.
Give Him your worries, for He knows you're confused.
His grace, His healing, His love for you is true.

Separation Anxiety

Nothing can separate us from God.
The world will not come between His children and His love.
Nothing we say or do will leave us abandoned.
There is room for each of us in His mansion.

Can you imagine loving someone like that?
Always stepping to the plate and taking their turn at bat.
Can you imagine never turning your back and walking away?
Even when there is deceit, anger, or rage.

It may be something we will never fully understand.
God is here always, even in sinking sand.
We may never be able to comprehend
the gift of love, through Jesus, that God has sent.

> Nothing…in the whole world will ever be able to separate us from the love of God. (Romans 8:39)

The Mask I Wear

When I am missing my father,
tears may come to my eyes.
I will stuff those tears back,
therefore, everyone sees that I am fine.

This is my coping mechanism.
My thought is someone may need me.
So do not give it away that I may not be okay.
I will put on this mask for everyone to see.

Can I let others see me for me?
Do I take off this mask, and let myself grieve?
It is hard, when life just keeps going, to stop and take time.
So I keep working and focusing on other things, instead of me.

I am limiting the power of my Lord Jesus,
not trusting in Him for all things and leaning on myself.
So I ask myself, "Do I truly grasp that He has power over everything?"
Jesus, help me, because I am weary of carrying this grief on my own.

Help me, Lord, take off this mask and cry in Your arms.
I pray this to You, Jesus, my Savior.

Thinking of You

As I look to say goodbye,
through tears and sorrow, I cry.
I know that you are at peace,
and your suffering has been relieved.

Memories of a lifetime together,
bring a smile that will last forever.
Pictures stored in my mind
of all the laughs and good times.

Although this is your final curtain call,
I know you'll be watching us all.
As the seasons, like the wind, come and go,
you'll smile and watch your grandchildren grow.

When someone says, "That's just what mom would do!"
I'll cherish knowing that part of me is from you.
I'll see you again, although I don't know when or how.
It's a moment in time to say goodbye, for now.

This Is My Prayer

May the Lord watch over you while I'm gone,
reassure you we'll be together later on,
hold you in His arms while you cry,
for it is time for me to say goodbye.

This is my prayer for you, my wife:
Lean on our Lord for comfort and never lose your love for life.
Continue to walk and trust in our Lord,
and again one day, like eagles, we'll soar.

Know that I will always be close by,
in your thoughts, your heart, I'll even hear you sigh.
My love, our memories, are in your heart to stay,
'til we see each other again one day.

May the Lord Jesus hold you in His loving arms.
May He keep you safe from all harm.
This is my prayer, as my life on earth is done.
My love will surround you 'til again one day we are one.

Welcome Home

Your life has been a tribute to your faith in Me;
My love, through you, radiated for all to see.
When your body grew tired, your steadfastness never wavered.
There was no doubt to anyone I was your Savior.

Relax now and let my arms wrap around you, to bring you home.
Those you left behind I will never leave alone.
No need to look back, your work there is done.
It's your turn to bask in God's glory—to sit at the feet of the Son.

Welcome home, for life on earth is complete.
Welcome home—sit and rest, while I wash your feet.
Welcome, faithful servant, to My heavenly choir on high.
Welcome, My son, to My mansion in the sky.

Welcome home!

When I Think of You

It's been two years since I said goodbye—
when I need comfort, I look to the sky.
The warmth of the sun is your love
as it shines on me, from heaven above.

Our daughter is growing older;
I tell her things you would have told her.
When across the hills thunder is rolling,
she smiles and says, "It's just Dad, bowling!"

When I remember your presence and grace,
I look at our child and see your face.
A child of hope, love, and determination—
a future leader of this nation.

When things in my life go wrong,
I lean on the love we had to keep strong.
Having you in my life, I was blessed.
I'll see you when I come to my final rest.

Where Are You, Lord?

I need answers to my questions, Lord!
How can I keep my feet moving forward?
You have left me here all alone.
Why don't you just take me home?

Come on, Lord, I can't hear you!
Can't you see I'm too tired to see it through?
Nobody will even know I'm gone.
So let me be with you, my Holy One.

Is it part of your plan I was left behind?
Don't you see I'm going out of my mind?
I'm waiting patiently to hear your voice.
I know that ultimately it is your choice.

My Child, can you not feel my arms around you, my presence near?
Have you not faith that I will overcome all your fears?
Do you not know what a precious gift you are to me?
I am with you now and throughout eternity!

Why?

Sometimes I just don't understand why.
Why does someone so young have to die?
Why is there pain?
Why is there rage, then someone is slain?

Help me to at least try...
to understand why.
I alone am not capable or strong enough.
I need You, Lord, to surround me with Your constant love.

I've tried to be good, I've given it my best,
I work so hard, with little rest.
My faith and trust are in You.
Only You, Lord, can see me through.

No matter what I will have to face,
You are there with Your saving grace.
These trials on Earth will not capture me—
in You I have been set free.

Nature

A Little Seed

A little seed in the ground
is waiting to be found
by the sun and the rain,
to rise up to its fame.

If the ground is made of sand,
there is no place for its roots to land.
It withers and it dies,
before it has time to try.

Rocky ground is even worse.
The seed from the beginning is cursed.
Nowhere for it to grow,
it lies and waits to sow.

Dark rich soil a seed does love.
It bathes in the sun and rain from above.
It flowers and grows,
its true beauty it shows.

Stillness of the Morn

A rustle of a doe in the brush.
The wind's gentle hush.
The birds waking in song.
Footsteps of a fisherman, walking along.

The sun breaking over the hill.
The waters, quiet. Still.
The grass wet from the morning dew.
I sit and watch the day start anew.

The freshness of the crisp, morning air.
The dampness of night, lingering everywhere.
I pause to give thanks to my Lord above
for sending these signs of His love.

The Evening Glow

The evening sun glows orange in the sky,
Canada's wildfires are burning in forests nearby.
The smell of wood and haze reside in the air,
wildlife goes on without a care.

A rabbit eats the tall grass near the gate,
a hawk flies over, looking for dinner before it gets late.
A mother and her spotted fawn come to graze in the meadow,
the sun fades, and the earth is enveloped in shadows.

The day is ending, only a few hours are left.
The moon and stars will shine where the sun has set.
The good news is God's promise for another new day
gives hope to the weary, as we kneel to pray.

A new life, a new day Jesus has given.
So rejoice, come alive, and in His name start living!

The Morning Awakes

The lake waters calm, smooth as glass.
Birds singing or digging for bugs in the grass.
Four deer with two yearlings, feeding on the church lawn.
A gray squirrel, playing chicken in the road, as I travel on.

You are the one Lord who created all things.
Your creation awakes with praises, and sings.
Sprinkles of rain fall down from heaven above.
The warm morning air encompasses me with Your love.

Each new day brings reminders of God's grace and wonder.
The earth awakes, revealing God's splendor.

Under God's Sky

Getting away from it all…
hearing the Lord when He calls.
Taking the time to get away,
under God's sky for just a few days.

Letting your problems go…
listening to the wind blow.
Out under God's big starry sky,
watching the world go by.

Everyone needs this quiet time
to look up above for His sign.
Everything will be alright,
under the sky so bright.

Camping with new friends,
hoping the fun never ends,
realizing it's for a few days.
Thanking God for the time to get away.

Wings of a Dove

When you're tired and lonely,
with nowhere to turn,
just look toward heaven,
and you can learn.

To trust in our Father,
in Heaven above.
Just let yourself be carried
on the wings of a dove.

For in this life we are given hope,
if we trust in the Father, Son, and Holy Ghost.
Know that no one is without God's love,
just kneel down to Him up above.

Let yourself be carried
on the wings of a dove.

New Year

Fresh Start

This is the time of year we long for a fresh start.
Baby Jesus came down to heal our broken hearts.
The Messiah's love came to heal everyone's pain,
to cleanse our souls from a life that is stained.

For a people who are torn and tattered,
Jesus was born to collect the scattered.
Taking the weight of our sin, we can start anew.
His life brought hope and forgiveness to see us through.

Bringing peace, joy, love, and happiness,
Jesus was born and mankind was blessed.
Out of love, God sent us His only Son.
Jesus was born, our Redeemer, the Holy One.

He will take away grief, sin, and fears,
His love will dry up all your tears.
A baby, the Savior, will bring a life that is new.
A fresh start is waiting for you.

Like New

Like a New Year's fresh start,
Jesus can heal a broken heart.
Helping with all of life's pain,
He cleanses a soul white from all stains.

He can take away all fears,
and wash away all tears,
giving us a chance to start anew,
like the air of a brisk morning, covered with dew.

Jesus will take charge of a life that seems tattered;
He collects all the pieces that seem scattered.
Jesus is offering a life that is brand new.
Be accepting of Him today, and all the year through.

Happy New Year!

Personal Tributes

Eye on Her Savior

Today, Molly finds peace and rest.
Against cancer she gave her best.
Through it all, she never lost sight of her Lord.
Walking with Jesus, in eternity, is her reward.

Molly showed others how to live.
Her loving heart to others she would give.
Never wavering in faith, she gave her life to the Lord above.
She showed others how to live in the Savior's love.

Molly's light shone forth from her beautiful soul,
never questioning that God would make her whole.
You see, God's answers and ours sometimes don't match.
We want healing here, but God's healing was calling Molly back.

Back to Him, her Creator, her Redeemer, her Friend.
Going home, being with Jesus in eternity, where there is no end.
Molly has lived her life to claim that prize.
Jesus gave all of us that choice when on the cross He died.

Dying for every one of us, Jesus can set us free.
Molly knew that, Molly lived that, Jesus's face Molly now sees.
Hope is not here with anything on this earth.
Hope is in Jesus, who became man through virgin birth.

As we remember Molly and say goodbye,
remember her legacy is that on Jesus she kept her eyes.
With eyes on her Savior, her light shone.
Jesus answered her call and brought her home.

Grandma's Faith

Grandma's love for Jesus radiated for all to see,
her childlike faith was an inspiration to me.
Grandma's love of her family was constant and supportive,
her walk with Jesus showed us how to live.

Her eyes were always on Jesus above,
showing the world His wondrous love.
All of us that knew her, our lives have been blessed.
She showed, in life and death, true grace and happiness.

In her death, she was not alone,
Jesus was there to welcome her home.
In heaven there is a grand celebration,
for Grandma has reached her final destination.

Leader of Faith

Ray Taylor was a leader in church and a good friend.
He was a blessing to all who knew him.
Some say with his love of God he should have been a preacher,
but Ray's calling was to be a junior high science teacher.

Always thanking his Lord for life and each day,
he ended his day on his knees to pray.
For in Christ Ray put his faith and trust;
he lived life to the fullest, a lesson to all of us.

If you knew Ray, you find strength in his life.
He was a leader of men, keeping Christ in his sight.
He loved his Lord, and in Him he did stand,
which comforts us now to know he is in God's hands.

See You Again

When he left, he handed out a holiday embrace.
I hope he knew what he meant to our workplace.
Always laughing and joking, in good cheer,
He said, "I'll see you again next year!"

With his smile he could light up the room.
His love of life could end my gloom.
My body was numb when I heard the news,
that Pedro will not be back any time soon.

His life cut short, like a blink of an eye,
his next plane is heading to heaven, in the sky.
I feel blessed in knowing this lovable man,
and ask God for help to understand.

Sixty Is Old in Any Language

Sixty is old in any language.
You realize your life is changing;
your body is tired and sagging,
your face and eyes are bagging.

Wrinkles are on more than your face,
they seem to be spreading all over the place!
Instead of your children chasing you,
your grandkids have you running 'til you're blue.

The oxygen in the air is awful thin,
as you tire easily and suck a lot of wind.
You used to welcome large, noisy crowds,
now you can't wait to be away from anything loud.

You'd rather sit and think about the past;
family gatherings are no longer such a blast.
Memories of what you did five minutes ago are gone,
but boy, your memory of years ago goes on and on!

Sixty is old, no matter how you say it!
You're happy your body keeps moving, bit by bit.
Although you're not that same young man,
I am still one of your biggest fans!

This poem I dedicate to you, Uncle Fred.
This family has been blessed by the life you've led.
Laughter and joy you have brought.
When we needed a smile, it was you we sought.

Prayers

A Prayer

Lord,

You are the source of all our hope,
equipping Your people with the power to cope.
In a world filled with disappointment and ridicule,
You unite us in faith, to keep us renewed.

It is by living our lives, in Your grace,
those around will see Your face.
So help us to stand for that which is right,
as we pray to You for wisdom and insight.

So as we come to worship and praise You this hour,
lift us up, Lord, and fill us with Your awesome power.

Amen.

A Prayer for Believers

God of steadfast love and grace,
heal our hearts, as we celebrate You in praise.
Your mercy draws us to gather here.
Your peace and understanding extinguish all our fears.

As we come together to thank You for Your wonderful deeds,
help us to know You are in control and will take the lead.
Reign in us so we can soar like eagles, taking flight,
showing the world that, in You, there is new life.

Grant us wisdom and courage to walk in Your way.
Dwell in us, oh Lord, for we need You each day.

Amen.

Before You

We come before You, Holy God, with many needs,
calling to you to help us, please!
We may be in the fight of our life,
not knowing how we will get through the strife.

Battles are around us we may not win.
Help us to remember to cast our eyes on Him.
Give us peace that passes anything we understand,
trusting in You that this is part of Your plan.

Lift us out of our ruts and routines,
that life may not be as bad as it seems.
There is a reason for us to celebrate each day,
to be thankful we have You to show us the way.

Help us to praise You for each day we are given,
by walking in life with You, knowing our destination is heaven.
There is fullness in life with You.
We are never alone—You are always there to see us through.

Amen.

Glorifying You

Open my heart that I may see
the woman You are praying I would be.
Lead me to walk always by Your side,
that Your will not mine, I always abide.

Help me, Lord, to always be Your light,
so in a world of darkness, my life for You shines bright.
Use my life as a testimony to Your mercy and grace.
When others see me, they know my life is in the right place.

A place of peace and forgiveness, which comes from accepting You.
Living my life to give You glory in all I do.
When I stumble or fail, my Lord picks me up.
He surrounds me, and I bask in His love.

I pray to You, my Lord and guide.
Let me never stray too far from Your side.
Help me to remember my life is to glorify You.
My reward is with You, in heaven, when my life here is through.

Thank You, Lord Jesus, Savior of my life.
I love You with all my heart.
Yours forever…

Praying Us Through

Lord Jesus,

As we reach out to touch Your face,
let us be reminded of Your love and grace.
When we're troubled and live in fear,
wrap Your arms around us, dear Jesus, and hold us near.

Help us to remember someone is praying us through,
feeling comforted that You watch over all that we do.
Always holding us in Your mighty hands,
and, when needed, carrying us across the sand.

Let the candidates and team feel Your awesome power,
as we pray for them this holy hour.
May they experience a love that is like no other,
while forming new kinships with their new brothers.

Let each one look upon you with new sight,
feeling refreshed and basking in the warmth of the Son's light.
Taking with him a life that feels brand new,
always remembering someone is praying him through.

Amen.

Your Glory

I give thanks to You, Lord, as I kneel at Your feet,
for promises in my life You continue to keep.
You show me glimpses of Heaven above,
Your glory surrounds me in continuous love.

With every single blessing,
Your strength is beyond my understanding.
In every instance, I see Your wonder
beyond what my mind can ponder.

You travel with me down every road,
helping me to carry every load.
I am nothing, Lord, when torn apart from You.
Teach me to show Your glory in all I do.

Thoughts and Reflections

All in My Mind

Have you ever been completely depressed?
Have your worries led to a lot of unrest?

I've often wondered how I deal with these feelings. Maybe I'll hope
they just go away.
We all know that this doesn't happen. We need to face them, learn
from them, and keep going in spite of them.
A lot has happened to me this past year. I know I'm stronger because
of it, but I still look back and wonder, *Why me?*
It's time to look to the future, to set goals (even small ones), so my
accomplishments bring positive reinforcement to my life. It's
time to come out of depression and reach toward tomorrow,
with confidence and guidance from my Lord Jesus.
I used to tell my late husband, "If you get out of bed with your mind
set on feeling lousy, that is how you're going to feel. Wake up
each morning thankful for a new day." I guess it's time for me
to live what I preach.
After all, it is all in my mind how each day will turn out. A positive
outlook is always a better way to look at life.
Thank You, Lord, for insight and patience.

Be Still

Be still, and know that I am God.

—Psalm 46:10 (NIV)

What power is in those words. Be still! When was the last time we just sat still? Or did we say, "Not now, Lord. I don't have time"? Like a young child, full of energy, we can't seem to find the time to fully reflect on God. Maybe you're like me. If I sit too long in one spot, I tend to get sleepy, and my eyes start to close. So instead of reflecting on God, my mind begins to nod. After a short time, there's no sign of life because I'm down for the count!

So how do I "be still, and know that He is God"? Let me think about this…

I know! How about those twenty minutes I drive to work every morning? Instead of cranking on the radio, I could choose to be still. I could talk to God and, most importantly, listen to Him.

How about when I take my daughter to dance and have an hour wait 'til she's done (because it makes no sense to go home)? I could really get some quality time in there, just my Lord and me.

What about those five to ten minutes throughout the day in between what I just finished and my next project? Just "Be still and know that He is God."

In looking at my day, I think there are probably a lot of times when I could be still but choose to do other things. In today's society, it's the American way to always be on the move and be involved in all that we can. The funny thing is, no matter how busy I become, God is still here today, as He was yesterday and will be tomorrow. So, I can outbusy myself and avoid Him or I can *be still*, focus, and rejoice in knowing that He is God.

One Grace Card

When we have differences with one another, are we not to give grace to the one who wronged us, and try again? Are we not to try to mend fences and find common ground? Do we only give one grace card, two, or maybe three? How many is the right number? It breaks Jesus's heart, and my own, for someone to say enough grace has been given. Our spirits should be uneasy with this message. Jesus's heart breaks when grace is not given or only in small amounts. His heart breaks when there is turmoil between believers.

Step back. Think about your own life, your life in Christ. If you could only have one grace card from Jesus, would it be enough for you? Would two or three? Would Jesus's death on the cross then mean nothing, as there would not have to be that much grace? Do we not, each of us, have several sins for which we could use grace? Our Savior died for all those sins so that His grace would be enough for each of us. Do our lives not have to reflect our Savior's? How then can one grace card be enough? How can even two or three? Grace should flow through us to others just as Jesus shows us His daily grace. His grace is as far as the east is from the west. Should we not try to do the same?

> *But God, being rich in mercy, because of the great love with which he loved us, even when we were dead in our trespasses, made us alive together with Christ—by grace you have been saved—and raised us up with him and seated us with him in the heavenly places in Christ Jesus, so that in the coming ages he might show the immeasurable riches of his grace in kindness toward us in Christ Jesus. For by grace you have been saved through faith. And this is not your own doing; it is the gift of God, not a result of works, so that no one may boast.* (Ephesians 2:4–9 ESV)

Intoxicated with unbroken success, we have become too self-sufficient to feel the necessity of redeeming and preserving grace, too proud to pray to the God that made us. (Abraham Lincoln)

About the Author

For the past several decades, Lana Keller has discovered comfort, joy, and healing though writing Poetry. Her words, inspired by her Lord, seek to lift the hearts and souls of her readers in hopes that they too will see him in a new light. She is a mother, grandmother, basketball coach, small group leader, and actively pursues Jesus alongside her church family.

www.ingramcontent.com/pod-product-compliance
Lightning Source LLC
Chambersburg PA
CBHW021213130726
47988CB00002B/638